Facebook Marketing

The Only Facebook Marketing Book You Will Need!

Increase Sales by 30% by Using These Facebook Marketing Secrets!

A Complete Guide!

Table of Contents:

Introduction

I want to thank you and congratulate you for downloading the book, *"Facebook Marketing: The Only Facebook Marketing Book You Will Need! Increase Sales by 30% by using These Facebook Marketing Secrets! A Complete Guide!*

This book contains proven steps and strategies on how to utilize Facebook marketing strategies to promote your business and boost your sales.

Social media has taken the world by storm and business should acknowledge the fact that they can reach more clients and have greater conversions when they utilize the power of social media. Facebook is the largest and most popular online platform in the world today and it is certainly the best place to advertise your business or brand. It boasts of a billion users – think about the great potential that is in your hands when you launch your advertising campaign using Facebook Marketing. Moreover, Facebook has different tools and utilities available to you to create optimal engagement with your existing client base and potential market.

With Facebook Marketing, the possibilities are endless. Start your marketing campaign today!

Thanks again for downloading this book, I hope you enjoy it!

responsibility or blame be held against the publisher for any reparation, damages, or monetary loss due to the information herein, either directly or indirectly.

Respective authors own all copyrights not held by the publisher.

The information herein is offered for informational purposes solely, and is universal as so. The presentation of the information is without contract or any type of guarantee assurance.

The trademarks that are used are without any consent, and the publication of the trademark is without permission or backing by the trademark owner. All trademarks and brands within this book are for clarifying purposes only and are the owned by the owners themselves, not affiliated with this document.

Chapter 1: What Is Facebook Marketing?

When social media networking began, MySpace was the most popular platform with more than a hundred million active users. However when Facebook came into the picture in 2008, it triggered the decline of MySpace.

You may be thinking that if something as big as MySpace could be displaced, the same thing might happen to Facebook after a few years when something bigger comes along – so why should you make an investment in Facebook Marketing? For one, MySpace only reached a hundred million users, but Facebook has almost a billion to its name, making it the most visited website of all time. In the US alone, there are 150 million users – you can imagine the potential of reaching an unprecedented number of potential customers.

Understanding the Whole Thing

Facebook marketing is, in simple terms, marketing via Facebook. It is all about developing and actively utilizing a Facebook page to promote your product, service or company. You will use the Facebook page as a communication tool to connect and engage your customers.

Facebook provides not just individual personal profile pages but also business pages that groups or organizations can use to create a fan base for their brand.

Because of the potential billion-customer reach, everyone who wants to make their brand known should use Facebook for their business.

Since social media has become mainstream, having a business Facebook page has become as important as a business website. Different sectors are making use of Facebook Marketing:

Local businesses

Family-owned businesses, online shops and even franchises of bigger companies use a Facebook fan page to get people to know more about their store and spread the word to others.

Brands

Popular brands are promoted through Facebook pages, from home goods, foods, restaurants, electronics, retail stores – almost everything is on Facebook. The business pages are being used to inform existing customers of current product developments, promotions or special deals. When active fans like, share or comment on the posts, they are effectively promoting the brand to other passive and potential clientele.

Personalities

Celebrities use Facebook pages to connect with more fans and make themselves even more popular. You will find actors, directors, musicians, authors, news anchors, and anybody who has a name or wants a name.

Public service and non-profit organizations

Charities, churches and even political groups use Facebook to publicly spread their various campaigns online.

Demographics and other Important Information

Facebook started as a social media outlet for college students, but it has developed through the years and become an effective marketing tool for different kinds of users and customers. Since Facebook has a significant number of users, you can reach a wide variety of markets. Studies show that a large percentage of Facebook users belong to the 18 – 25 and 26 – 34 age group. They comprise more than half of the Facebook population. The next largest group are those who are 45 – 54 years old, followed by those who belong to the 35 – 44 age group. A good 8 percent of users are teenagers (13-17) while the remaining 5% are those aged 55 and up. This means that Facebook reaches a diverse demographic and business can take advantage of that information.

It is also important to know when Facebook Marketing will prove to be most effective for you. Research shows that when posts are made in the morning, they are more likely to engage many people and get more likes, shares and comments compared to those posted in the afternoon. But of course, it depends on what kind of business you have and what kind of audience you wish to target. For instance, you need to understand that if your clients are usually at home, they check the Facebook accounts during the day – usually from 3:00 pm onwards – and morning is the best time to post so you can reach them. On the other hand, if your target audience are those who go to school or work, they only have time to check their Facebook accounts before they go out of the house or when they get home. If this is the case, you will lose opportunities by only posting in between 9:00 am to 5:00 pm.

How to start a Facebook Marketing Campaign

A Facebook page is almost always linked to a business website or blog. To make your Facebook page more effective, you need to use the exact information in all your online sites. You want your existing clients and potential customers to be familiar with you and your brand, using different names or titles for different pages will defeat the purpose.

The first thing you need to understand about a Facebook business page is that it is different from a personal profile page. With a business or fan page, you don't have friends and you can't invite people to be friends.

The Facebook business page will have fans. To start your fan base, the first people who need to like your page should be you and your marketing team. If you are a big enough company, all your employees should be encouraged to like the business page. There are two ways to increase the fan base. One, your initial fans can invite their friends to like the page. Two, once a fan likes your page, your post will be added as an event to their personal profile. This event can be seen on the newsfeed of their other friends who will then hear about your brand and like your page as well. It works just like the conventional word-of-mouth advertising.

Improving your Facebook Page

One of the most important, if not the most, factors that make Facebook marketing effective is consistent communication. It is not enough to create a page and expect your fan base to grow without doing anything. You should consistently post a variety of content that is new, fresh and relevant. The more people see your engaging posts, the greater the likelihood that they will share your page.

Content generation is just like conventional marketing. You can announce new products, upcoming promotions, have client testimonials, offer discount codes and the likes. What is important is you keep your fans interested in your Facebook business page.

Keep in mind that every user that likes your page will automatically receive notification of any new content that you post. If they are interested in what you posted, they can either like or comment on it and their action will reflect on their newsfeed, to be seen but all their friends. They may even share your post. You should encourage this cycle to continue as this kind of passive marketing will help you reach more people and build your fan base.

Once your Facebook business page is set-up, you can add variety to it to make it more appealing to your fans and potential audience. You can download different apps that will allow you to do the following actions:

- Link your Facebook page to your YouTube channel if you have one

- Link your Twitter account and business blog

- Improve engagement by adding a raffle to your page

- Generate leads by allowing your visitors to sign-up for newsletters

- Get customer feedback

Why should you post often? An average

user may have about 130 friends and be a fan of many other groups or brands. The more often you post content, the more recent you will appear on his newsfeed. If you don't post regularly, your fans may not see your activity instantly on his newsfeed and you will lose engagement. Again, you want people to see your posts and be visible on their newsfeed.

You can also build your fan base and strengthen your client engagement through low-commitment investments such as polls and contests and adding calls to action on your posts. When you engage your audience often, you are encouraging affinity you're encouraging affinity your brand and establishing yourself as familiar to your client base.

Moreover, responding to queries and comments made on your posts promotes two-way communication. Keep in mind that good customer service means customer retention. So don't lose the opportunity of serving your clients well by interacting with them through your Facebook page.

Facebook Marketing Strategists

You can do Facebook Marketing by yourself but if you have the money to employ a social media marketing strategist, you can utilize Facebook pages even more. There are a number of marketing people you can employ to manage your Facebook page and other social media platforms such as an

Internet Marketing Manager, Marketing Manager, Advertising Manager and a PR Manager. Normally, the job description of your social media marketing staff comprise the following:

- Encourage company engagement through social media

- Develop videos and other content to be shared

- Create marketing slogans on brands, products or services

- Direct particular promotional assignments

- Write press releases, spotlight stories, and related narratives

- Analyze trending attitudes and

consumer behavior

- Organize and manage different internet marketing campaigns

- Institute marketing goals and assess success using measurement tools

- Oversee internal and external marketing strategies

Chapter 2 - Reasons Why You Should Use Facebook to Promote Your Business

Marketing is important to any business. Success comes when a product or service is promoted at the right time in the right way to the right audience. Facebook is a way you can share valuable business information to a greater audience and meet business objectives. Facebook is a great platform to market your business because it is the biggest leading website on the planet today. Facebook has 1 billion users and counting – 500 million of them are active. More than half of these active users log on to their accounts on a daily basis at least once a day. Often average users will access their account multiple times in a single day, creating at least ninety pieces of content every month as he shares posts, links, photos, etc.

These users interact with a good number of groups, pages and events. One user can be associated to at least 70 groups, pages or events. Research also shows that a user will have an average of 130 friends meaning you will be able to connect to that 130 other users by reaching just one.

You need to capitalize on these facts – Facebook connects people and businesses. If you use this to your advantage, you will experience your brand becoming more popular through "Likes" and "Shares" compared to using traditional promotional materials. A single like from a user is equivalent to a personal referral that will increase awareness of your product or service. Facebook is interactive and more personal compared to a professional business website. It is easier and less complicated to share posts, photos, videos and the likes. Facebook can be customized optimized without much technical expertise.

Another reason why you should use Facebook is that it is very easy to register for an account – and it is free! It is a no-cost way to get to where your existing customers and potential future clients are and connect with them.

Advertising via your Facebook page is

also less expensive compared to traditional advertising. When people like and share your posts or your page, you can raise business awareness – it is like a multi-level marketing strategy.

Having a Facebook page will give you the opportunity to direct your clients to your business page as well as gather more leads.

Facebook allows business owners to interact in a more personal way with their clients. Businesses can respond more quickly to their client's needs and queries. When clients are satisfied with customer service, brand loyalty increases.

Chapter 3 - How to Utilize Facebook for Marketing and Promotion

Once you understand how powerful Facebook Marketing is and how it can benefit your business a great deal, you will immediately want to sign up for an account and start connecting with your clients. Before you do so, you need to determine if your clients are on Facebook. If you are involved in retail and you serve consumers, you will most likely find that your existing customers and potential clients are on Facebook. Since they are, then you should be on Facebook, too, because it is a way to reach them. Your customers most likely expect your product or service to be on social media so they can connect with you or talk about you.

Setting Up your Page

Keep in mind that, in the social media community, your Facebook page is the face of your business. It is the extension of your physical business. It can make or break your business. You need to consider the following:

- You should be discoverable. Your profile should be one that is easy to find when people start looking up your business name.

- Your page should have insightful and timely content. You are regularly reaching different people in large numbers. You should have posts that meet their needs and satisfy their interests.

- It should be personal. People should feel connected to you through your page. This means that they know they can have one-on-one conversations with you when they need to know something.

When you are already on Facebook, here are the things you need to do:

- Let people know you are on Facebook.

- Once you are on Facebook, you

should let your clients know. You can place a link to your Facebook page on your business website, blog or other social network sites like Twitter. You should also include your Facebook link on your printed marketing paraphernalia.

- There are three ways you can make your page known so you can start building your audience. One is to invite your friends and ask them to show their support by liking your page. Another way is to share your page using your personal Facebook account. Lastly, you can invite your existing clients and business contacts through email.

Make sure your profile will attract clients.

Use your business logo or product images as your profile picture. Make sure that our profile information is complete – include your business page's URL and add a brief yet informative and interesting company overview. Use this page to provide a description of how your product or service can help your target audience.

Utilize the power of SEO

When people search the internet for products or services, they usually use keywords. To make your Facebook account end up high in search engine results, use keywords in your Facebook posts and profile information.

Make sure your posts attract people

Do not post boring, technical information. Instead, put out content that will attract people to click the "Like" or "Share" buttons and make comments. Keep in mind that most people are visual and they prefer images over mere words. You should also consider compelling yet positive content – posts that bring out human emotion in an encouraging way. However, you should be careful about posting anything that is not in line your company values.

Your business can come alive through compelling content. Post photos, updates or links that are inspiring. The key is to be genuine. If you are only sharing posts just because they are viral and you are not genuinely happy about them, you may lose client engagement sooner or later. People know when you are just after clicks or you really want to encourage them.

You need to be consistent

You should post regularly because it will connect you more with your audience. It won't take too much of an effort on your part if you will set a schedule for your posts. Having a regular schedule will keep you in touch with your audience and they know when to expect a post from you. As you are consistent, your followers will trust you more.

Connect with your followers

When followers make comments or post queries, it is important that you respond to them. This will give them the impression that you are real and that you listen care. Remember that Facebook is a great way to get customer feedback which will help you improve your business. Additionally, positive engagement will cause other people to endorse your business. If, however, you need more time to make a response, you should still let your audience know that you are working on it.

Make sure you direct Facebook traffic to your business website or business blog

Your main objective is to urge people to visit your business webpage and make conversions via a call to action. If you have a blog, you should adjust your settings in such a way that it will publish clips of your blog on your Facebook page. This way, you will encourage Facebook followers to click on the feed and visit your business blog.

Offer rewards

Let your followers feel that you appreciate them. You can conduct raffles, competitions and special promos that are exclusive via your Facebook page.

Study Page Insights

You can try out different types of posts – from photos to testimonials to updates – so you can see which ones your audience prefers. By looking at Facebook's Facebook Insights, you can check the overview provided and measure your engagement with your followers. You will be able to assess if your Facebook ads are supporting your business objectives and make adjustments as necessary.

When you identify what works, replicate that success. If your audience engages more when you post photos, for instance, then continue to post photos. Understand that when people like your post or share it, your audience becomes bigger because their friends – who are not yet your followers – can see the post and have the opportunity to connect with you. When you have a successful post, promote it so you can reach more people and get more conversions.

Keep in mind that Facebook is an excellent platform to reach people who matter to your business – let it serve you well. You should recognize and understand your Facebook followers and potential audience, create an engaging business page profile, connect with your followers in every way through posts and comments, and never ignore feedback.

Chapter 4 - Tips for Effective Facebook Advertising

Facebook marketing has amazing capabilities that can successfully aid you in reaching your target audience. You can tailor your message, create more engaging posts by using images and more. Here are some tips that will help you create effective marketing campaigns using your Facebook page, help your Facebook page grow, attract more followers and stay engaged with your fan base.

Make your posts short. In today's world, a lot of people have little time to spare and you should apply this principle to your ads. Make your posts brief and straight to the point. An ideal post should be about 100 to 250 characters. Facebook users don't go much for novel-like posts unless you create a catchy enough headline that will cause them to rethink their schedule and give you the time of day. For optimal engagement, keep things short and simple.

In posts that have images, keep texts to a minimum. Image-based ads should only have no more than 20% text on them. Make sure that your texts are as catchy as the images.

Update your cover photo from time to time. Cover photos can reflect seasons in your business. Changing your cover photo from time to time will show your audience that you are active and you want to keep with the times. You can also change your cover photos if you are hosting a contest or having a special sale. It is a good way to advertise your event.

Make use of Facebook tagging. This is especially helpful when you are working with other brands, groups or organizations. Include tags in your Facebook posts to extend your exposure. For example, you are hosting a promo and giving away items from a particular company, tag that company so you can also reach their fans. Other things you can tag include your clients, conferences you attend, pages of businesses whose photos, videos or articles you share. They may even tag you back which will put you in the limelight as well.

Jump in the #hashtag bandwagon. Just like with Twitter, you can use a hashtag to promote your campaign, product, service or brand. If you have a Twitter account, you can also connect your marketing campaign with Facebook using similar hashtags. You can get fans involved by inviting them to add hashtags to encourage conversations.

Don't go easy on images. People are visual and studies have shown that Facebook posts and ads that contain photos get more engagement compared to posts and ads made up of words. Use images to make your advertisement stand out.

Use large images. Billboard advertisements attract greater attention and you can use the same strategy in Facebook by using a bigger social media picture instead of the automatic generated link on your post. You have different options:

- Use a text ad with the auto-link

image box using a small image

- Add text to a bit.ly link and use a larger photo as a separate image post.

- Insert text to the bit.ly and create a custom image. Overlay text on the photo.

Bring variety. Remember that multiple images do the trick. You can use as many as six images in your Facebook ad.

Use quality resolution for your images. Do not upload grainy or blurry images. It is recommended that you use

1200x627 pixels for your advertisement.

Utilize the power of YouTube. YouTube videos create serious engagement so if you want connect with your audience, use them. Just make sure that you do not post anything that will come against your company's ideals and reputation.

Keep valuable content cryptic. People are naturally drawn to the mysterious so it will be a good idea to hide valuable content as in a barrier. This will cause viewers to go on your page and like it in order to read more. To make it more interesting, you should include an attractive graphic, good headline or copy and an appealing call to action.

Check out and use targeting options so that you know what to post. Demographics are according to age, gender, location, relationship status, residence, education, workplace, language, etc.

Once you identify your ideal audience, you can **utilize Facebook's interest targeting**.

Cater to the needs and interests of your existing fan base but also build on new ones. By using targeting options, you can create posts that serve to reach three groups: those already connected to you, the friends of your existing fan base, and those who are not yet connected to the page.

Check the potential audience meter. The good thing about Facebook targeting options is that it gives you a picture of the potential audience you can reach. While it may only be an estimate, you will get an idea of you are narrowing your audience or you are targeting too many. You can narrow you reach using the "More Categories" option. Under this section, you can add topics such as those who post using a lot of images, those who have birthdays during the month, etc.

Use Facebook Offers to draw in clients to your store or official business website. You can give away coupons that clients can redeem in your store or when they make a purchase online via your web page.

Make use of your existing mailing list and build from there. You can easily upload it to Facebook by using Mail Chimp.

Let other people help you. If you are not that big of a business and you don't have enough funds to hire a Social Media Marketing personnel, you don't have to do everything. You can ask someone you trust to be an administrator to handle your Facebook ads account, edit promotions and stop ads when needed. The administrator needs to have his own Facebook account or is a friend of yours on the platform.

Here's how to add the administrator:

- Click Ad Manager

- Go to Settings

- Click Ad Account Roles

- Click Add User

- Choose access level

- Click Add

Use bidding options to control advertisement costs to your advantage. There are different bid setups you can select such as clicks, particular objectives and impressions. If you will choose the default bidding option, for instance, which is the one based on your desired objectives, you will have less customization compared to bidding for impressions or clicks. It all depends on your marketing goals. Select between daily and lifetime advertising budget. Facebook allows you to set up a daily or lifetime budget. The daily budget controls your daily marketing campaigns. In essence, this means that your sponsored stories will cease from showing on the side column and newsfeeds once you reach your daily budget. This is good if you have a limit on advertising costs but it may keep you from reaching a greater audience. On the other hand, the lifetime budget helps you decide on the amount you spend over the whole span of your campaign.

Facebook advertising campaigns run on separate budgets, so remember to spend within your financial comfort zone.

You can **create an ad** even if you don't have a Facebook page. If you don't want to have a Facebook business page but you want to cash in on Facebook marketing, then you can make an ad via the Clicks to Website or Conversions objective. However, your ads will not appear in newsfeeds. They will only be seen in the right column.

Change details on your advertising campaign when needed. Facebook allows you to change the end date and the daily ad budget of your advertising campaign. So if you see the need to adjust, based on reports and feedback, do it.

Chapter 5 - More Ways to Use Facebook for Marketing

The value of Facebook for marketing cannot be exaggerated. Among all the other social media platforms, Facebook holds the number 1 spot. It is not just a place for friends to connect, it is also a venue for brands to promote themselves and interact with their clientele. It doesn't matter if you are a big business or a small brand, you can use a Facebook fan page to make yourself known, increase your audience reach and build customer relations.

Here are some ways you can use Facebook for marketing and promotions

Use the Facebook fan page to create awareness for your brand identity

Conventional marketing strategies make clients familiar with business brands through product and services listings. With Facebook, you can promote your brand through a customizable page that expresses your business's unique character. You can share posts, images, videos and links that show your personality. Compared to formal business websites, a Facebook page is more personal and can express your human side. People will easily identify with you because you are not just a business who is trying to take consumers' money.

You can be flexible when it comes to creating brand awareness and affinity through Facebook. The posts you share can either be related to your product and services or not at all, as long as you are connecting with people and not diverting away from your company's philosophies and core values. You can share funny videos, viral posts, educational references and the likes.

Use Facebook Ads

Similar to classified ads in newspapers, Facebook has its own way of promoting brands. When you advertise, your ad will be seen on the side column of the social media site. These ads include the following features:

- Headline

- Copy

- Image

Click-through link to your Facebook page, official website or an app

When you have an advertisement on the side column, you are increasing your chances of page visits, website clicks and possible likes.

- When you use Facebook Ads, you will be able to do the following:

Target particular audience according to demographics. You can utilize information such as age, gender, and interests among others.

Set your own budgets for advertisements. These can be on a daily, weekly or monthly basis.

Test ads. You can run multiple versions of your ads at the same time. You will be able to compare your setups and designs and see which is more effective.

You can measure your own ads using Facebook Ad's built-in tools.

When you use Facebook Advertising, you increase the likelihood of generating "Like" on your page. Once a user likes you page, they automatically become followers and your posts will be visible on their newsfeed. When they like your post, that event will be visible on their friends' newsfeeds. This means more interaction and further reach which may mean possible conversions.

Host promotions, sweepstakes and contests on Facebook

Like conventional marketing, promotions can boost brand awareness. You will be using a third-party app to make a contest and direct participants to your Facebook page. The reliable contests are not simply asking for participants to like your page or writing a comment. If you want their entries and your contest to be valid, use other tools and contest templates. There are free tools like Shortstack and Pagemodo but you can also use a lot of paid tools.

Use promoted posts

By paying a flat rate, Facebook will allow you to have promoted posts that reach specific number of users. This ensures that your follower and fans ALWAYS see your post on their newsfeed. When you don't use promoted posts, the chances are high that your post will be swamped by others and you will lose visibility. Additionally, Promoted Posts also allow you to the friends of your fans.

You can set up Promoted Posts with just a click of a button. You don't have to worry about computing how much you pay on a daily, weekly, or monthly basis because it comes with a flat rate. However, it does not include the options for targeting that you can use with

Facebook Ads.

Use Facebook Sponsored Stories

This is all about word-of-mouth advertising. Sponsored Stories encourage users to imitate the action of their friends on Facebook. For instance, if a friend likes a page, then he will think it is a reliable or interesting site and will like it as well. If a friend claims an offer from a Facebook page, the user may also be enticed to do the same. Even if the friend has liked the page a long time ago, the user will still see it on his news feed and on the right column. This way, the post does not get overlooked.

Sponsored Stories can also be utilized

with Facebook's Open Graph. For example, a friend has just played and installed a particular game on Facebook, the app will send an invitation to challenge friends to play the same game. Sponsored Stories are easy to create and customize.

Use Facebook Open Graph

Effective marketing relies on studying your client's reactions and interactions. The same is true with Facebook. You can see billions of different kinds of user interactions daily using Open Graph. This helps you identify other creative options that you can utilize for your posts.

Third party apps often prompt users to register using their Facebook accounts and it automatically connects them to Open Graph. Once they sign-up or login using Facebook, the app requests permission to other applications. Usually the user just clicks through this without giving it much thought. This way, the apps are able to stream information onto other friends' newsfeeds, such as what song the user is listening to, what movie he is watching, what game he is playing, etc. This gives the friends various options like action, do the same action or share it. It capitalizes on consumer story, like a testimonial.

What makes Open Graph actions effective as marketing tools is that they are more meaningful. When a familiar friend is sort of promoting the brand in a particular way, users are encouraged to take action.

Use Facebook Exchange

Ad retargeting is possible with Facebook. Businesses can analyze web history data and see when a user has visited their webpage but did not make a purchase. If this is the case, they post an advertisement for the same product to reach the same user to encourage him to click that Buy button. It is interesting to note that FBX can also appear in newsfeeds aside from side columns.

With all these amazing ways you can

advertise, Facebook is the best social media network to promote your product, service or brand.

Chapter 6 - Attracting Your Target Audience and Avoiding Ineffective Facebook Ads

Facebook marketing is very versatile and it offers different kinds of businesses and brands many options to boost their advertisements as well as reach particular related demographics and interests: the target audience. It is easily the most important aspect of marketing. Businesses should first identify who they want to reach and where this audience is before they can begin to formulate marketing strategies to reach this audience. Facebook marketing is effective at identifying the demographic profile and geographic location of the target audience. With demographic targeting, you can indicate the exact city, country and radius of the audience you want to directly engage.

Facebook ads allow you to optimize tools that can fine-tune your search through a number of different interests such as age, gender, preferences, income status, and even insurance status. For example, you can find 30-year old males who live in Minnesota who have a car insurance policy and does yoga. This can be possible because Facebook gathers the information in a person's personal profile. Moreover, in partnership with Epsilon, Data Logix and Acxiom, Facebook can pull together other personal and financial data that may not be on Facebook. While it may sound quite uncanny, it is a strategic move.

You can use this information to your advantage: fine-tune your demographic search so you can create effective and engaging ads purposely targeted to your specific audience.

While it may cost you extra for marketing expenses, you need to realize that it will be your dream audience that you are reaching. That particular group that can spell success for your business. Instead of just garnering many likes and shares from users who will not convert to potential customers, you can focus your efforts on reaching people who will actually become clients and bring sales in.

Additionally, Facebook allows you to measure the effectivity of your ads through its black and white reporting. You will be able to gather the following information and see if the effort is paying off:

- Frequency of ad

- Audience reach

- Start and end date of your ad

- Particular cost per ad

Let's say you would like to increase traffic to your website to 50% in a month. You can set your marketing budget at $ 2,000.00 and assign an average cost per click of $ 0.24. You may get about 500 clicks at the end of the month. Thee information will be valuable when you are setting your budget for the next month. You will also be able to identify if your kind of ad is effective or you need to use different ad sets.

Tips on Avoiding Ineffective Ads

Poorly constructed advertisements can harm your brand image. Ads that have misspelled words or pixelated images can turn potential clients off. Make sure that you have compelling, interesting and appealing ads with these tips:

Use high quality images.

You want to look professional, not cheap. When you use pixelated images, people will not be attracted and will not want to visit your page again. Always use your own quality images. If you are going to use stock photos or share other people's images, make sure they have high resolution. As much as you can, avoid images that are blue because they don't stand out in the Facebook newsfeeds.

Use videos

Videos are fast becoming the mainstream media. You can have a Youtube channel and create link from your Facebook page or you can upload your videos directly to your Facebook page. You can also make use of Facebook Live to make your connection more real-time.

Again, it is good advice to stay away

from videos that feature blue and hues because you want your videos to be prominent and not blend in with the whole Facebook background.

Have a clear call to action

Remember that you are advertising to get people to do something that will benefit you – like make a purchase. You need to give them a good enough reason to click on your advertisement and visit your Facebook page. When people understand why they are going to click on something, they will most likely take immediate action. You can entice them to respond to a call to action by asking questions and answering their queries with a strong and positive response.

Always keep in mind that using all capital letters and more than two exclamation points can make your ads look like spam. You want it to appear personal and engaging so that they want to click on it. You can also use an image to indicate a call to action, but you need to remember that it should comprise only 20% of your ad's image.

Make a catchy headline

When people read a headline, it should cause them to stop and consider. You don't want them to just scroll past your ad as if they didn't see anything interesting enough that is worth their time. A good way to grab their attention is to ask a question that will make them want to read your whole post, view your image or watch your video. Once they take notice of you, you have the perfect opportunity to lead them to more clicks, direct them to your website and encourage them to respond to your call to action.

Make it a point to connect appropriately with your audience

Your posts, photos, videos and copies should represent your business or your brand well. You cannot just post unrelated images because you are building familiarity and affinity with your audience.

Understand your marketing goals

You need to identify your marketing goals so you can run effective ads. When you know what you want to accomplish, you will know how to do it. Here are some examples:

Do you want to connect with existing customers and brand your product through Facebook and other social media platforms?

- Are you looking for online leads or sales?

- Are you promoting a new event or an app that is related to your brand?

When you have answers to these questions, you will be able to create an effective ad and build a strong online presence via Facebook.

Remember that conversion happens on your website

Keep in mind that Facebook is a tool to get people to visit your website and respond to calls to action. Make sure that your Facebook posts and updates will direct your fans to visit your business website or landing page and encourage them to respond to your call to action. It can be subscribing to your business blog, filling up a contact form or making a purchase. To be able to analyze the number conversions that happen through your Facebook advertisement route, you can use tracking pixels.

While Facebook ads may increase engagement on your Facebook page, you need to make sure your ads builds up the traffic to your business website. But adding clicks to your website don't mean you should always direct them to a contact form page or a product purchase page. You should choose the best performing URL on your site. If for instance, your homepage is your most excellent page, direct Facebook traffic there.

Do not limit yourself

While newsfeed ads and desktop advertisement can be effective to a degree, you should also try mobile ads. Studies show that mobile ads are shared more often to be shared compared to desktop ads so don't limit yourself to the conventional and easy.

Moreover, when you advertise using Page Post Engagements, you can be assured that your fan base and the friends of your current fans will be able to see your posts and engage with you. Use Facebook targeting tools to help you identify specific demographics and interests so your posts can be more effective and increase client engagement.

If you don't utilize Page Post Engagements and Sponsored Posts, you may have very interesting posts and high quality images but only a few fans will see it and you will not actually reach your desired audience. It will just be a waste of time and creativity. While advertisements such as Sponsored Posts and Page Post Engagements may cost you money, make it an effort to allocate a fraction of your marketing budget for important posts that will allow you to interact and engage with more people. This will be especially helpful when you are holding raffles, contests or events – the more people you reach, the greater your turnout will be.

Conclusion

Thank you again for downloading this book!

I hope this book was able to help you to understand the great potential of Facebook Marketing and how it can bring great success to your brand or business.

The next step is to apply the strategies, techniques and tips you learned from this book in order to build a good fan base, reach your target audience and create conversions. Learn to use bidding options and set the advertising costs that are suited to your financial capabilities. You can create an effective marketing campaign through Facebook and see great returns on your investments. There is no better time to start than now!

Finally, if you enjoyed this book, then I'd like to ask you for a favor, would you be kind enough to leave a review for this book on Amazon? It'd be greatly appreciated!

Thank you and good luck!